THE ULTIMATE GUIDE TO PEPPER SPRAY

HOW TO CONFIDENTLY CHOOSE AND USE THE BEST LESS LETHAL DEFENSE

DAVID NASH

Copyright © 2019 by David Nash

All rights reserved.

No part of this book may be reproduced in any form or by any electronic or mechanical means, including information storage and retrieval systems, without written permission from the author, except for the use of brief quotations in a book review.

CONTENTS

PLEASE REVIEW

This book is dedicated to the first postman to carry pepper spray, as it was the post office's use of OC spray as a deterrent to animal attacks that caused the FBI to officially classify pepper spray as a chemical agent in 1987.

PREFACE

Since you are reading a book on self-reliance, I am assuming you want to know more about how to take care of yourself in disaster situations

I would like to suggest you take a moment and visit my website and YouTube channel for thousands of hours of free content related to basic preparedness concepts

Dave's Homestead Website
https://www.tngun.com

Dave's Homestead YouTube Channel
https://www.youtube.com/tngun

Shepherd Publishing
https://www.shepherdpublish.com

INTRODUCTION

If you asked me who I am, I would answer that I am a Dad. Being a family man is the most important aspect of my life. Providing for and protecting my family is what I see as my highest purpose. Luckily my career has allowed me to gather the skills and information to be able to effectively protect my family from the threats in life.

You see, I am a long time firearm instructor, a former US Marine, and a preparedness advocate. I have written several traditionally published books on firearm usage and disaster preparedness. This is my first self-published book, but I have taught this subject for nearly 20 years.

I own a private training school called the Shepherd School[1]. It originally began as a firearm school, but as my skills and certifications grew, so did my understanding of what it meant to protect my family. Guns are only one aspect of true preparedness and protection. I have to be able to bandage a wound, teach my child how to stay out of trouble, know how to put out a kitchen fire, get my family to shelter during a storm, and change a flat tire. Being the family protector is more than just being able to employ deadly force. I have that option if I need to use a gun, but what about those that can't carry a firearm, or don't want to?

My wife is a special education teacher. She couldn't carry a gun to work even if she wanted to. She doesn't want to. Unless someone was trying to hurt our son, I am not sure she could even draw a gun against another human. I wrote this as a guide for people like her. I want to give you some quality guidance on how to buy, carry, use, and decontaminate pepper spray. I make no judgments on your choices. I just want to help you feel (and be) safer.

I have been a pepper spray instructor for almost 17 years. My first experience with chemical agents was in 1993 when I entered the Gas Chamber at Paris Island. A year or so later I received my first dose of pepper spray while trying to impress a girl by showing off. She had a little can her daddy gave her when she went to college, and I wanted to show how it was not nearly as powerful as the stuff we used in the Marines. I was wrong on both accounts, she wasn't impressed and I learned the power of good pepper spray.

Later I became a correction officer, and then a chemical agent instructor. Over the years I have lost track of how many times I have been sprayed. I've been sprayed a lot, whether for training, or as a side effect of wrestling with someone being sprayed it hurts and is not fun. Currently I work as correction academy instructor, and we spray our cadets as a part of their formal pre-service training. With the understanding that comes from thousands of exposures to pepper spray as the person spraying, being sprayed, or helping decontaminate the sprayed individual both in and out of classroom settings, I can confidently say I have a good understanding of the mechanics of pepper spray usage. I also know what does doesn't help make it stop hurting.

I can also say I have heard almost every conceivable bad theory on pepper spray. This short book is designed to separate the rumors from the facts and to give the best advice possible.

WHAT IS PEPPER SPRAY?

Without going deep into the history of pepper's being used as a weapon, dried pepper powder was used by Japanese police in the mid 1800s to blind criminals.[1]

They used a small box with a mouthpiece to blow pepper powder at suspects. Our technology has greatly improved, and the formulas now contain the extracted chemical rather than just being a solution of ground pepper plant.

The active ingredient in pepper sprays is called oleoresin capsicum (OC) this chemical is extracted by using a solvent like ethanol and then the solvent is evaporated leaving the OC resin.

The resin is then suspended in a carrier liquid like water, oil, or alcohol and placed in the spray container. A propellant gas like butane is then used to pressurize the container so that the liquid can be expelled at an attacker.

Some formulas use flammable carriers or propellants that can be ignited if an electronic device like a stun-gun or TASER is used after OC spray exposure. Most OC manufacturers now use water instead of alcohol as a carrier liquid and inert gas such as nitrogen instead of butane as a propellant. However, many law enforcement agencies still test for flammability.

Oleoresin Capsicum is an Inflammatory Agent

OC is not Mace, Mace is a brand of chemical agent. The two less lethal chemical irritants (tear gas) in use are CS and CN.

OC is an inflammatory agent. It works differently.

CS Gas is actually a compound mainly used in military tear gas grenades. It is called 2-chlorobenzalmalononitrile.

CN is Phenacyl chloride and was invented in 1965 when a chemist's wife was threatened on the street. This turned into the Chemical Mace brand of self-defense sprays.[2]

It is important to know that CS and CN sprays are chemical irritants, they hurt, but it also takes some time for them to begin irritate the exposed person, so it takes a few seconds for them to begin to feel the pain. Chemical irritants are also is harder to decontaminate than OC.

OC is an inflammatory agent, it hurts of course, but its true purpose is to cause exposed mucus membranes to swell. This causes the eyes to swell shut so that an attacker cannot see. If the spray gets into the nose it makes it hard for the attacker to breathe.

If a person cannot see and is fighting to breathe, then their effectiveness in attacking the citizen is reduced considerably.

Add in the pain factor and many people panic when sprayed. An attacker in a mindless blind panic can be dangerous, but it also can allow you time to remove yourself from the situation.

Because OC is an inflammatory and not an irritant, it begins to work instantly when exposed to mucus membranes. As soon as it gets in the eyes the eyes swell shut and begin to hurt.

OC is also easier to clean off (decontaminate) than chemical agents. This is important in the even you get contaminated during a fight. For law enforcement agents it is vital because they arrested suspect can't be booked into jail until they are decontaminated and shorter clean up time means more time on patrol.

Some companies sell blends of OC and chemical agents, even including dyes for marking suspects. I have used OC/CS blends with some success, but I prefer stronger straight OC sprays. My preference is to have a spray that hits hard immediately, so I can get away or gain control, and then decontaminate rapidly so I don't have to suffer any longer than I have to (in a later section I will explain why I worded that as I did rather than say so the attacker won't suffer longer than necessary). Remember the justification in using OC spray is not to hurt people, but to render them less capable of hurting us.

Before we get into the strengths, types, and sizes of OC defensive spray options, I think it is vital to have the understanding of a good defensive mindset.

ARE YOU SURE YOU WANT TO CARRY PEPPER SPRAY

There are a few different reasons to carry Pepper Spray – You may carry pepper spray because you have a specific fear. That fear may be an angry ex-husband, protection while jogging, just in case… You may carry because you don't like guns, are afraid of guns, or you can't own a gun because of your age or other reasons. You may carry spray because it is not lethal and you are unwilling or unable to use deadly force. Some, like me, carry both a gun and a can of spray to have the flexibility of a two tiered response.

In the end it does not matter why you carry defensive sprays, as long as you understand the laws of using force and are willing to actually employ the tools you have. I work inside a prison as a trainer of new staff, so I am familiar with the common criminal mindsets. I know first-hand how effective felons are at reading weakness. If you choose to carry a defensive tool of any kind, you must first decide to use it if needed and to determine what actions would cause you to respond with force.

As my primary defensive tool is lethal, I have decided exactly what would cause me to potentially kill someone. I would not shoot a person over stuff. I would hand over my wallet to an armed robber in an instant, but I would kill or die before I would let them take my son as a hostage. A burglar can take my TV and leave, but if they approach the bedroom hallway I would respond with force.

I do the same type of contemplation with my spray, it is less than lethal, so the mental preparation is not as intense, but you should understand, that when you are involved in a fight you never know how it will turn out. For myself, I would never spray someone simply because I was mad at them, or they "creeped me out," but I would spray someone that grabbed me, tried to pull me into a dark alley, or tried to strike me. If you are in a threatening situation, you don't have time to think about cause and effect, you should already be familiar the law, understand justified self-defense, and know your capabilities.

If you are dependent on the tool to scare an attacker a way and don't have the fortitude to actually employee the device, an attacker will know that will respond accordingly. The answer to a criminal's question of "what you going to do with that," should be a strong, confident, and firm "Spray you if you don't stop!"

In short, don't carry it if you won't use it, and if you use it make sure you can explain why.

The legal standard for use of pepper spray is much lower than that of a gun, which makes it a valuable option. Most states do not regulate the ownership of pepper sprays, or have legal age limits for carrying. This is much different from handgun carry. Only one state in the US has no legal statute describing how to legally carry a handgun (Vermont).

In my state, for example, it is legal to use force to stop a theft or terminate a trespass, but you cannot use deadly force or even the threat of deadly force to do so. So, in Tennessee, if I caught someone stealing I could use OC spray to make them stop stealing. However, I would be committing a crime if I shot them, or even threatened to shoot them.

3

—————

WHAT IS THE PROPER MINDSET?

Whole books could be, *and have been* written on the proper defensive mindset. Based on my experience and training, the right mindset is much more important that any tool you have at hand.

A proper mindset is noticed by attackers and often causes them to find an easier target.

First, and as we covered earlier, if you are going to carry a weapon, then you must be 100% willing to use it when needed.

Next you need to be smart. Know the law and understand what the reasonable man standard is.

If you have any defensive firearm training of any sort, you have to have heard the term "Reasonable Force" at some point. The reasonableness standard is probably the most important test when someone is trying to decide if your defensive action is justified or not.

However, you may ask just what is reasonable?

This is a large part of any self-defense training I provide because I believe it is a lot easier to teach an individual HOW to shoot than it is to teach the WHEN to shoot.

Each state has its own laws, and since I am a trainer and not an attorney so I cannot give you a legal opinion on the law, but based upon my training and experience as a firearm instructor I can give you some points of consideration for you to research on your own.

I also feel the need to inform you that my training is geared more toward armed professionals (Law Enforcement and Security), and that the majority of legal case law that I know is geared toward them. However, I do believe that many of the lessons learned from police shootings apply to civilians as long as the armed citizen understands the entire situation, including the legal differences between LE and citizen.

In my security classes I talk a lot about Tennessee vs. Garner[1] and Graham v. Conner[2], but they are just the starting point for learning about legal use of force.

We know that no single person is perfect, and as a group we are not perfect. There is no real person that we can hold to be perfectly reasonable 100% of the time, but by creating the legal fiction of a reasonable man. Our legal system can use this fiction as an objective tool to avoid subjective decisions. This creates a system where the law works in a foreseeable, uniform and neutral manner when attempting to determine fault.

The reasonable person standard assumes that each person has a duty to behave as any reasonable person would under the same or similar circumstances.

The law cannot predict specific circumstances of each case, but the reasonable person standard does not change. You have act in a reasonable way, no matter what is happening.

The question that I s used to decide the reasonableness of an action is; would a reasonable (non-emotional) person, in the similar circumstances, with similar training act as you did.

This is not democratic, it is not about comparing your actions to that of the average person. The average person may be wrong (look at the last couple elections or the ratings for reality TV). The fictional Reasonable Person is not emotional nor subject to personal whim.

The Reasonable Person is Defined as:

The reasonable person is an ordinary, prudent person who normally exercises due care while avoiding extremes of both audacity and caution.

Used as a test of liability in cases of negligence, this standard is not applied uniformly on all persons because varying degrees of reasonableness may be expected from a minor (infant), an adult, an unskilled person, or a professional such as a doctor. See also prudent man rule.[3]

For citizens, it is important to know that you do not get to decide if your action is reasonable. Of course you think your action was right, otherwise you probably would not have done it.

The first person to decide on the reasonableness of your act will be the responding officer, then prosecutors, judges, the media, your family, friends, and the general public.

Considerations for the Reasonable Person:

- What is the foreseeable risk of harm his actions may create against the utility of his actions?
- What is the extent of the risk he is going to create?
- What is the likelihood such risk will actually cause harm to others?
- Are there any alternatives of lesser risk, and the costs of those alternatives?

Taking such actions requires the reasonable person to be informed, capable, aware of the law, and fair-minded. Such a person might do something extraordinary in certain circumstances, but whatever that person does or thinks it is always reasonable.

This is pretty hard for the average person to live up to without a certain amount of preplanning, training, and serious thought.

You are a reasonable person, so you have thought about your situation and made decisions you can explain. You know why you decided to carry OC spray instead of a gun, or OC Spray and a gun. You read the instructions on how to use it; you may have even practiced using your tool, or even taken a few classes.

Awareness is a Large Part of Proper Mindset

We aren't talking about guns specifically, but when I train people in firearms I point out that if you choose to carry a gun, every fight you get into is a gunfight because the person you are fighting may try to take your weapon?

This idea applies to anyone that decides to carry a defensive tool; even a less lethal one like OC spray or a TASER, you must stay aware of your situation and what is around you.

In my book **Handguns for Self-defense**, I spend a lot of time discussing mindset and awareness and because it applies to all manner of defensive tools and actions I will cover it here.

Two basic mental tools can help a person understand situational awareness. While they both describe the same idea the same way, you rarely hear of them at the same time.

These tools are the color code system popularized by the late gun-training icon Colonel Jeff Cooper and the National Rifle Association awareness levels as taught in their Personal Protection in the Home curriculum. For purposes of clarity, I have included them both in the following chart.

As you move up the levels of the chart, certain changes take place. This happens because the more your mind becomes ready to fight, the more it prepares your body to fight.

At this time, all you need to know is that the higher you move up the levels of alertness, the less you are able to perform complex tasks or critical thinking. If you have ever been unexpectedly scared and get jolted to the point where you are not sure what to do then you have experienced the flight/flight/flee response. The more levels you jump at a time, the slower you are to respond and the greater impact will be to your body.

It is easier to get ready to fight if you are expecting a threat. It is harder to make good tactical decisions when you are surprised and have to jump from being unaware of a threat to being ambushed by it.

Condition White/Unaware

In condition white you are going with the flow, unaware of anything outside your immediate human impulses. Basically you are unaware of what's going on around you. You are not ready. This condition, sadly, is the one most citizens live in for their entire lives. There are some situations where this is unavoidable. Sleeping, for example, is an activity where it is impossible for you to be in a higher level of awareness. While there is no moral connotation of evil attached to this level of awareness, it is not the proper mindset of a person concerned with his or her own safety. Anytime you are outside your home you should strive to not be unaware. This is especially true if you feel the need to carry a defensive tool like OC Spray. How can you justify carrying a weapon and not staying aware of threats?

Condition Yellow/Aware

If you are in condition yellow, you are alert, but are also calm and relaxed. In this level of awareness, you are scanning your surroundings for threats. You know who's in front of you, to your sides, and behind you.

It is important to understand that at the awareness level you are not anticipating an attack, but you are mentally ready in case of one. With practice, you can maintain this level of awareness for extended periods of time.

This is the best compromise between readiness and exertion. Higher levels of preparedness are meant for actual threats and not for long term.

Condition Orange/Alert

If you go to condition Orange, then you have a specific sense of unease. Something is not right. Something has alerted you to danger. Perhaps there are a number of suspicious men standing around your car. Or in the classic Jeff Cooper example, a guy wearing a raincoat comes into your shop on a sweltering summer day. What's wrong with this picture?

In the Orange level, you are aware of the positions of all potentially hostile people around you, as well as any weapons they may be able to use, either in their hands or within their reach. You are developing a plan for dealing with the potential hostilities: "...first I spray the guy walking toward me, and then I run north away from his friends standing around the park..." You may have also identified escape routes, depending on what response you will use. In addition to being mentally ready, you are physically ready as well.

In the NRA system at this level, you have pre-decided "trigger-points" that cause you to move to the next higher level of awareness. I whole-heartedly endorse this type of thinking. At this level of stress, it is hard to make complex decisions, especially when your decision involves life and death consequences with their respondent legal ramifications.

Condition Red/Alarm

If you are sitting at the Alarm phase then the fight is on. You are being actively attacked. There is little time for thinking or second-guessing your decisions.

Do what you need to do to survive.

There are only three ways to prepare for this: practice, practice, and practice. Bruce Lee once said, "I fear not the man who has practiced 10,000 kicks once, but I fear the man who has practiced one kick

10,000 times." You have to burn your actions into your muscles so that when the time comes you don't have to think about how to run your gun.

Remember when you first started driving. It took thought to start the car, to put it in gear, to navigate through town. What would have happened if a dog ran out in front of you your first week of driving? After 10 years or so of driving every day, has it changed? Do you have to think about starting your car or do you just get in and drive?

If you're going to fight, you do not have time to figure out how to draw or what your sight picture should look like, you need to be in the fight.

Time Critical Decisions

Once you understand the importance of defensive awareness you should start to learn how to make decisions under stress. One well-used tool comes from the military and is called the OODA Loop.

In the 1950's a young USAF fighter pilot named John Boyd, who was cocky even by fighter-pilot standards, issued a standing challenge to all comers: starting from a position of disadvantage, he'd have his jet on their tail within 40 seconds, or he'd pay out $40. Legend has it that he never lost. His unfailing ability to win any dogfight in 40 seconds or less earned him his nickname, "40 Second" Boyd.

While undoubtedly this Air Force pilot had a high level of skill with his fighting tool, what made him great was that he knew how to make decisions quickly and accurately under stress.

The Air Force was so impressed with his skills they had him create a formal briefing to share this knowledge with the other pilots. This short briefing turned into a larger course taught at the Air Force Academy.

His system has been partially credited for the outstanding success of the American fighter pilots in the Korean War. Colonel Boyd's system is called the OODA Loop. OODA is simply an acronym for Observe, Orientate, Decide, and Act.

- *Observe* - A creepy guy is always in the park where you take your daily run.(Yellow).
- *Orientate* - Is he approaching you? Is he a threat? (Upgrade to Orange), or is he homeless or waiting for someone (stay at Yellow)?
- *Decide* - Does the situation call for force, retreat, or no action? What are you going to do in the situation? How are you going to do this? If you followed my earlier advice and created pre-designated actions based upon certain "trigger-points" your response would be made even faster.
- *Act* - Do it! Act decisively and with purpose. I have seen a lot of people hurt because they took "Half-steps" because they were afraid of getting into trouble.

The OODA Loop explains the mechanism of decision-making. The basis of how it applies to self-defense is simple. Once you understand how your attacker makes decisions, you can get inside his OODA and do things that force him to reorient himself so that you can gain a speed advantage.

Basically, you want to make your attacker react to you rather than play catch-up to him. Instead of allowing your attacker to act, change the environment to force him to reorient himself. If you are able to do this, it will seem like your attacker is moving in slow motion because you will begin to act while he is reacting to you. This can be easier said than done, but it is an area that deserves attention.

If someone thinks of you as a harmless object to control, and you respond with confidence and force (and the appropriate tools) then you effectively "get inside their OODA" it will force them to reconsider their approach....

It takes longer to react than to act

The main purpose of all this awareness and decision making talk is to help you create a reactionary gap. No matter what level of awareness you start at, when attacked you are going to jump automatically to

Alarm/Red. Imagine being awakened to a man on top of you with a knife to your throat.

This is a classic example of a condition White to Red response. Being more aware allows you to RECOGNIZE a threat while there is still time to take appropriate action (note, this is not always force; sometimes the appropriate action is leaving the scene, or even submitting). Whatever you action you choose, you will need time to implement it.

If you have created those mental trigger points, have confidence in your skills, awareness of your surroundings and situation; you are way ahead of the game. So much so that in all likelihood any potential criminal can tell you're not an easy target and will not put you in the situation to start with.

Could I Spray Someone?

Being prepared to act violently is not the same as wanting to act violently. One of my favorite quotes is from John Wayne in the movie *The Shootist*, "I won't be wronged, I won't be insulted, and I won't be laid a hand on. I don't do these things to other people, and I require the same from them."

90% of us live by some version of the Golden Rule, and are good guys at some base level. Don't forget that some people in society are bad people that like to do bad things. We need to cultivate a defensive mindset. Responsible people should determine in advance the level of force they are willing to use against someone who is attempting to harm our family or ourselves. Being ready to protect a loved one is not the same as wanting, desiring, or planning to kill.

I will not train someone who wants to hurt innocent people. I can't teach someone that doesn't understand the difference between justified and unjustified force and is not willing to learn. I preach avoidance, preparedness, deterrence, and that force is a last resort. I also believe that if it gets to the point where force is necessary, you must use enough of it to end the incident. Failure to follow through and end the attack will only cause more suffering and pain.

Andy vs. Barney

My mother once said that a lot of today's problems could be solved if school kids watched 30 minutes of the Andy Griffith show each day. I think she's right; there is a lot of good tactical knowledge to be gained from this old show. I use the Barney/Andy analogy quite often in my law enforcement classes.

It seems like in almost every episode of the Andy Griffith show a bad guy laughed at Barney, or Barney negligently fired into the ground trying to quick draw his pistol? On the other hand, Sheriff Taylor stopped almost every crime without using his gun?

That's TV, and isn't 100 accurate to real life, but the difference of mindset and the reaction people gave the two is realistic. That difference is based upon confidence. Andy did not need to prove how tough he is, he knew exactly what he can do, so he does not need to prove it at every chance. Barney feels like he gets his authority from his weapon, so he uses it like a crutch.

A can of pepper spray is just a high-powered hot sauce. It's your mindset that makes the difference. You build that mindset by training and deep contemplation on what you would or wouldn't do to protect you own or your loved one's life.

4

─────

COPS ARE SPRAYED DURING TRAINING,
DO I NEED TO BE?

Whenever I am either taking or teaching a pepper spray class I always hear at least 10% of the class comment that the reason they have to get sprayed is so that everyone knows how it feels like so that no one abuses the spray. That might not be the exact words used, but the idea that security or law enforcement has to feel the pain caused by pepper spray so they don't become abusive annoys me.

First off, if this is true, why stop with spray. Let's shoot all the police when they are in training... I mean, if a police recruit learns firsthand what a .40 to the chest feels like, they won't be tempted to shoot the wrong person... (The argument doesn't make sense in this light does it)

Secondly, if a police administrator has to use pain to create empathy and prevent abuse then they hired the wrong cadet or retained the wrong cop. They need some serious revisions to their human resource policies and training standards.

There are two reasons someone that carries less lethal sprays or TASERS need to experience them in training (and one is a minor reason).

Law Enforcement/Security personnel may need to be able to testify that they have an intimate understanding of the effects, and by being able to say they have been subject to the effects themselves, they can show that while painful, less lethal options are much more preferable to baton strikes or bullet hits. Personally I don't worry about that – I am not an administrator and don't concern myself with what some government lawyer would say about my actions.

Frankly I would not use force unless it is needed, and am not the type to use more physical force than I felt was needed to control a situation.

The true reason I want my students to get sprayed in training is for their own protection. I have NEVER been in a fight involving spray that either I, or someone on my team did not get exposed. Sprays tend to cross contaminate anyone near the fight. If you have never been sprayed, you will not know how to react to being sprayed. In my first OC spray instructor certification, not only did we get sprayed, we had to find the door back to get back inside the classroom, find a box near that door, dig through it to find a handcuff key, confront and control a hostile subject, subdue and handcuff them, double lock and then unlock the cuffs, and then find our way to the restroom where we could finally decontaminate ourselves. That was not fun, and it was not easy.

After that, I know that if I have to fight someone after being sprayed, I will be able to. I know I can take someone down and handcuff them, even if I myself am half blind from OC spray.

This matters because I also know that spray is not some wonder tool that ensures compliance, I know how effective TASERS are, but also how fast I can recover from one after being hit. Because I have been tased 4 times, I know exactly what they do. I know that they require a solid hit to work. In short, by experiencing the force option personally, I grow my own confidence in my ability to work while gaining personal knowledge of the weakness of the particular system.

In the end, I guess the "we are getting sprayed so we know what it is like" is true on some level. Unfortunately the words may be the same, but the difference in perspective is gravely different and engender two different mindsets and end results.

5

WHAT TYPE OF SPRAY SHOULD I BUY?

Short answer, it depends. There are different strengths, formulations, sizes, and probably the most important spray patterns and types to consider. Each type has its own strengths and weaknesses so let's take a few moments to talk about Strengths and Spray patterns.

How is OC Spray Strength Measured?

There are currently three ways manufacturers promote the strength/concentration of their particular brand of OC spray.

- Percentage of OC
- Scoville Heat Units (SHU's)
- Capsaicinoid Concentration

These three methods are listed from least accurate to most accurate. Most all law enforcement agencies in the US only use Capsaicinoid Concentration as a method of determining how "strong" a spray is.

· · ·

THE PERCENTAGE METHOD measures the amount OC by volume in a given solution.

The Pungency (heat) varies from due to pepper type and quality.

Because of this it is possible for a lower concentration of OC in a solution to feel "hotter" than a higher OC concentration solution. OC percentage is not a reliable indicator of product strength.

In common terms, which is hotter to your tongue, a chili made with 50% beans and 50% sweet bell pepper or a chili made with 90% beans and 10% ghost pepper?

Lower quality manufactures can use the percentage measurement to mislead consumers.

Scoville Heat Units (SHU's) is a measurement of perceived heat when a pepper product is placed on the tongue. This measurement is based on a scoring system assigned by a panel of five tasters from the American Spice Trade Association. As a reference here are some common peppers and their SHU rating:

- Green bell peppers 0 SHU's
- Jalapeno 5,000 SHU's
- Tabasco 30,000-50,000 SHU's
- Habanero 250,000-350,000 SHU's
- Bhut Jolokia (Ghost Pepper) 1,041,427 SHU
- Carolina Reaper 2,200,000 SHU

Unfortunately, Since SHU rating is based on the perception of heat rather than an exact measurement, the rating could vary from one panel to another. I used to sell Fox Lab's OC spray in the early/mid 2000s and their claim to fame was their 5.3 million SHU rating. I have been sprayed by Fox Lab's sprays several times and let me tell you they are HOT. I was a strong believer in SHU rating until I learned about the more scientific Capsaicinoid Concentration measurement.

· · ·

CAPSAICINOID CONCENTRATION MEASURES the amount of the actual capsaicinoids in a product. This is the unit of measurement that is the most consistent and best representation throughout all grades of Oleoresin Capsicum.[1]

Major capsaicinoids can only be guaranteed through High Performance Liquid Chromatography (HPLC) testing.

When I left Emergency Management and went back to the Correction field I had to attend the basic correctional officer academy. It was there that I was introduced to the concept of measuring the concentration, and that the hottest available spray in our Department was called Sabre Red[2]. I asked how the 1.33 percent Sabre Red compared to the 5.3 Million SHU Fox Lab rating. Without missing a beat, the drill instructor said, "It is comparable".

As the group leader of my class, when it was time to get sprayed, I went first and when asked "regular or extra-crispy" I volunteered to take the 1.33 Sabre Red instead of the lesser formula.

As soon as the spray hit my eyes I raised my hand and said,"I have made a mistake, don't take the extra-crispy" the young guys in the class laughed and thought I was joking.

I was not.

Upon promotion to becoming an Academy Instructor I had a discussion with that particular Instructor and related that while it is technically true that a Geo Metro has 4 wheels just like a Ferrari, it is unfair to say they are comparable when asked which would be a good first car.

OC Spray Patterns

There are different delivery systems that have spray patterns that have specific strengths and weaknesses in areas such as distance, accuracy, wind resistance, and blowback.

OC Pepper spray manufactures typical produce two basic spray patterns and two additional delivery systems besides a water based spray.

They are:

- Stream
- Cone Mist
- Foam
- Gel

THE STREAM PATTERN has the best range, generally 12-15 feet. It looks like the solid stream from a water gun, so breezes and winds do not easily affect it. This means is it less likely to blow back in your face. The single stream makes it easier to aim, but aiming is more necessary.

The recommended spray method for a stream of OC is to arc across the eyebrows (ear to ear) with the spray covering the eyes as a primary target.

One thing to be aware of with a ballistic stream is the hydraulic needle effect. It is strongly recommended that any aerosol discharged towards the facial area be limited to a safe distance of 3 feet because the stream may have enough force to inject itself into the first layers of the eye leading to permanent injury. However, if someone is trying to kill you, and OC spray is all you have, then you may have no choice but to spray at the dangerous distance. If lethal force was justifiable in a situation, and this was all you had, then blinding an attacker could be legally justified.

THE CONE mist pattern is easier to aim, because it has a wider spray pattern and finer droplets than stream. It comes out in a tight group, but spreads wider as the distance from the can increases. Because of the fine droplets it only has a range of 8 to 10 feet.

This cone of mist creates a pepper spray barrier that can impact multiple attackers, but a mild breeze can affect your ability to hit your target, and may come back on the sprayer.

The recommended spray method for a cone mist is to spray with a controlled motion from nose to mouth. Once you spray to hit your target, move away.

Cone mist is best used indoors because of its weakness in the wind.

THE FOAM DELIVERY system has an effective range of 8-10 feet. It comes out like shaving cream. This is used because it has a much smaller chance of being inhaled and is easier to clean up areas after spraying someone.

The problem is that foam can be scooped up by the target and thrown back at the sprayer. It is also very slippery on waxed or linoleum floors.

OC Gel was designed to enhance OC foam; it is sticky and coats the target when applied. It has the longest range of any spray, 15-20 feet and the weight of the gel makes it wind resistant.

However, unlike foam that will drip down behind an attacker's glasses, gel sticks and will stay where it is applied.

Primary target is the eye; concentrate aim between the eyes to be sure both are covered

6

WHAT ARE THE LAWS ON PEPPER SPRAY?

I am not a lawyer, and laws change over time, but I wanted to give a brief overview of the specific state laws concerning OC sprays at the time of publishing. Please take a moment to review the specific laws of your state before you carry OC spray.

It is a federal offense to carry/ship pepper sprays on a commercial airliner or to carry it beyond the security checkpoint at the airport.

Pepper spray may only be used in situations involving imminent physical threats or fear of bodily harm and may not be used to prevent theft or in situations of verbal abuse.

US Pepper Spray Laws

Pepper spray can be legally purchased and carried in all 50 states. Some states do regulate the maximum allowed strength of the pepper spray, age restriction, content and usage.

Alaska:[1]

Cannot be carried in a school unless over 21 years old.

. . .

ARKANSAS:[2]

Pepper spray container must be less than 5 oz.

California:[3]

California Penal Code, Section 12403.7, as of January 1, 1996, and as a result of Assembly Bill 830 (Speier), the pepper spray and mace programs are now deregulated.

California Penal Code Section 12400 - 12460 govern pepper spray use in California. Container holding the defense spray must contain no more than 2.5 ounces (71 g) net weight of aerosol spray.

Pepper spray may only be used in situations involving imminent physical threats or fear of bodily harm and may NOT be used to prevent theft or in situations of verbal abuse.

Certain individuals are still prohibited from possessing pepper spray, including minors under the age of 16, convicted felons, individuals convicted of narcotic/drug addiction, individuals convicted of assault, and individuals convicted of misusing pepper spray.

A police officer may cite or arrest a person who does not comply with regulations stated on the pepper or mace product.

Florida: [4]

Any pepper spray containing no more than 2 ounces of chemical can be carried in public openly or concealed without a permit. Furthermore, any such pepper spray is classified as "self-defense chemical spray" and therefore not considered a weapon under Florida law.

Hawaii:[5]

Pepper spray container cannot be larger than 1/2 oz. License required.

Michigan:[6]

Michigan allows "reasonable use" of spray containing not more than

10% oleoresin capsicum to protect "a person or property under circumstances that would justify the person's use of physical force".

It is illegal to give a "self-defense spray" to a person under 18 years of age.

Nevada:[7]

2 oz. container limit on CS tear gas, pepper spray is exempt.

NEW YORK:[8]

OC can be legally possessed by any person age 18 or over. No more than 0.67% capsaicin content allowed

It must be purchased in person (i.e., cannot be purchased by mail-order or internet sale) either at a pharmacy or from a licensed firearm retailer and the seller must keep a record of purchases.

The use of pepper spray to prevent a public official from performing his/her official duties is a class-E felony.

New Jersey:[9]

Non-felons over the age of 18 can possess a small amount of pepper spray, with no more than three-quarters of an ounce of chemical substance.

North Carolina:

When carrying for protection against people, container cannot be larger than 5 ounces.

Washington:[10]

Persons over 18 may carry personal-protection spray devices.

Persons over age 14 may carry personal-protection spray devices with their legal guardian's consent.

Wisconsin:[11]

Tear gas is not permissible.

By regulation, OC products with a maximum OC concentration of 10% and weight range of oleoresin of capsicum and inert ingredients of 15-60 grams are authorized.

This is 1⁄2 and 2 oz. (14 and 57 g) spray. Further, the product cannot be camouflaged, and must have a safety feature designed to prevent accidental discharge. The units may not have an effective range of over 20 feet and must have an effective range of six feet.

In addition there are certain labeling and packaging requirements, it must state cannot sell to anyone under 18 and the phone number of the manufacturer has to be on the label. The units must also be sold in sealed tamper-proof packages.

7

———

WHY NOT JUST BUY WASP SPRAY?

I don't care what the news reporters, your aunt Mabel, or the guy down the street that used to be a cop tells you. Using wasp spray as a "cheap" pepper spray alternative is a terrible idea.

The self-defense training world has a lot of people that speak without understanding. I can't count the times I have heard things such as,"my buddy the cop said I should…" It is doubtful your cop buddy would testify in open court that he told you do something ignorant or illegal.

Some instructors or online content creators don't care about the quality of information and teach questionable material to make a few bucks on tuition.

On the subject of bad ideas, I read a lot of internet bloggers mention using wasp spray as a cheap alternative to OC spray. Using wasp spray against a human is using a chemical outside of its designed use and as such is against federal regulation. It is not a reasonable act, and you may be held liable for any injury from using something not safe for humans on humans.

Wasp spray is designed to KILL, it shares many characteristics and precursor chemicals with chemical weapons used for mass destruction.

OC spray is designed to be less than lethal and is held to be safe for use on people.

Now, realistically, if the deranged crack-head felon that lives near my land comes and attacks me while I am out working at the land and I have a can of wasp spray because I was cleaning out wasp nests, then I may use it as a weapon of opportunity. But that is much different from choosing to save a couple dollars by choosing to carry and use a poison instead of a tested product.

To illustrate the concept a little further, in my state it is clearly against the law to carry a club or baton for the purpose of self-defense. I don't recommend it, and I don't recommend carrying a bat in the car "just in case". However, I have a son in T-ball, and he has a bat, a glove, and a ball. We keep it in the car because otherwise they don't make it to practice. This isn't a "wink-wink" I found a way to bend a law, but an actual reality of my life. If I needed to use a bat to protect my family, I am confident in my ability to explain why the bat was there to a jury.

The wasp spray is an illegal substitute for OC spray, just as it is illegal to carry a bat for self-defense in Tennessee. I may be able to get away with either if the situation is such that it is all I have and I am justified in severely injuring or killing my attacker. However, a prosecutor and most likely a jury will look VERY closely at the circumstances. If I used wasp spray to save a few bucks then I will most likely pay severely for that savings.

8

HOW SHOULD I CARRY PEPPER SPRAY?

You should carry your spray in a way that is easy to access while being out of sight.

This means you should not stick a can in your pants pocket, you won't be able to get to it in a rapidly evolving attack.

I personally don't like sticking a small can on my keys.

Keeping it on my keys does ensure I always have it near by, but it's awkward to get the can orientated so I can spray it. I know some people really like it. If the convenience is important to you then I suggest you get a break away key chain. Also be careful to buy a can with a safety cap. If you ever accidentally spray yourself you won't question why.

If you carry OC spray while jogging, a great carry solution is a wrist holster.

They make several types, some are more stylish that the one pictured.

I have even seen a bracelet that contained a small OC canister inside the band. After researching it I decided it was a novelty, but the point is there are a lot of hands free devices designed to be worn while exercising.

The way I prefer to carry my pepper spray is in a holster on the belt. That's probably because of my corrections background, but its easy to get to, and I hind that in todays world of people living in condition white with cell phones strapped on like batman's utility belt, its rather inconspicuous as long as you are not constantly touching and fiddling with the holster. I have seen a lot of people talk about carrying the holster and spray upside down to make drawing faster. I can't fault the idea for speed. It is faster. However, as a bigger guy, gravity is not my friend. I carry mine right side up so it can't possibly fall out of the holster.

Most people I know that carry pepper spray simply put it in their purse. I know that's how my wife carries. That's probably the best compromise option. A woman almost always has her purse, the spray is concealed, and if some thought is put into where it is placed and not just dropped in the bag a can is easy to access. I, and many other instructors' recommend clipping it to an inside front pocket. That way it is at the top for easy and quick usage. Additionally, if you have long purse straps, you can place your hand inside the purse and hold on to the can with the purse still on your shoulder. That's great for those code orange times when you get a "creeper" vibe or just have a gut feeling that something is off.

No matter how you decide to carry the spray, make sure you practice drawing the can and presenting it to a target. What works well in theory tends to fail in the intensity of an actually attack if it has never actually had the kinks worked out of the system.

Also in with the carrying, this isn't something to get and forget. Cans expire, and they leak.

There should be an expiration date on the bottom of the can, If an expiration date is not presence I write a date 3 years past when I purchased it. I also look at the nozzle for signs of leakage.

In the department I currently work for we also weigh the cans upon issuance, at turn in, and after use. Few things are worse than needing your pepper spray and it dribbles out because it is almost empty.

9

HOW DO I USE MY SPRAY?

Remember, that pepper spray is a defensive tool. It is considered a less lethal weapon, but it is nevertheless a weapon. It should never be used as a punishment of for harassment. A person can make you mad, but spraying them just because of that will likely end in a charge of assault against you.

Now that the mandatory legal disclaimer is out of the way, if you do feel threatened start by first gripping the canister.

The best way is to wrap your hand around the can and using the thumb on the spray actuator.

This may feel awkward, but it allows you to reposition the thumb and use your fist should you have to use hand-to-hand defensive techniques.

It is also much more secure. Using your index finger on top to make the can spray feels more natural but it is much easier for an aggressor to rip the spray can out of your hand.

I know that sounds crazy, you may be thinking, "How can a person fight after being sprayed?" Believe me they can, I have the bruises to prove it. Never trust any tool 100% and always have a back up plan.

I have been sprayed many times, and as an instructor I typically have to perform self-defense maneuvers after being sprayed.

It hurts, and I am functionally blind, but if an old, out of shape, fat guy can fight after being sprayed, you must bet that a young motivated attacker can also.

Steps for Using Spray:

Give a verbal warning, it can give you confidence, cause an attacker to find easier prey, and it helps the reasonability argument.

A strong and forceful back off or I WILL spray you is what you're looking for.

Next aim for the face, the eyes specifically. If the attacker is taller and you can angle up into the nose the impact will be highly magnified. A slash across both eyes is enough, however, I know a particularly tough Academy Drill Instructor that does a "Z" pattern. They spray of across the eyes, down the nose, and across the mouth. That works well, but the more you spray the higher chances you will get exposed through cross contamination.

Your first action after spraying your attacker is to break off and add distance. Hopefully, you can gain enough distance that you end up at the local police department and he ends up in jail. However, sometimes things go wrong and the attacker is able to get close.

If that happens do not be afraid to strike your attacker with the can if the spray itself did not work.

In the pepper spray uses I have been involved in most times that that spray did not get the desired effect the officer involved shook the can up and re-sprayed the subject, they did so over and over. Spray, Shake, Spray, Shake, Spray, Shake, Ad nauseam.

If the spray did not work the first time, you may have not gotten it in the eyes. If the situation warrants, try again. However if a second spray doesn't work then a third fourth or fifth attempt is also unlikely to work.

I have dealt with inmates that after being sprayed, wiped their eyes with their hand, licked their fingers and said, "Ummm good". If that is the case, then go to plan "B". Specifically if your attacker does this I would suggest start moving rapidly in the opposite direction, or alternatively if you can't run away Bop them in the face with the bottom of the can....

Essentials of Using Pepper Spray:

- Always aim for the eyes and face.
- Be sure to spray the eyes, but more might not be better.
- A spray can take a second to take effect. The effect is instantaneous once it gets in the eyes, but if they were closed it may take a second to get in them.
- Spray from a distance and then move as far and as fast as possible.
- Never rub your own eyes.
- Pepper spray does expire.

10

HOW DO I DECONTAMINATE OTHERS OR MYSELF?

When my cadets learn they have to be "exposed" to OC spray they are universally worried about getting sprayed. I don't blame them pepper spray hurts. In all honestly I would always choose a TASER over pepper spray (and I've been tased more than a few times myself). However, from personal experience I have tried just about every method for taking the burn away. I have sold commercial decontamination wipes and sprays. I have poured milk all over my head. I have followed the procedures in a scientific paper published by the Poison Control Center using Milk of Magnesia, as well as all manner of soaps and shampoos.

In all seriousness, I can unequivocally state that nothing makes it hurt less.

As I will explain a little later, time is the best and most reliable way of relieving the pain of exposure to Oleoresin Capsicum.

Even with the most potent law enforcement 1.33% sprays after about 40 minutes I will regain full function. However, with the procedure outlined below, I can cut that down to about 10 minutes. 10 minutes of burning eyes is still a long time. To compare, while the pain is (at least to me) slightly less than the 50,000-volt electrical jolt of a TASER, a Law Enforcement TASER ride is only 5 seconds.

Why Do I Have to Know How to Decontaminate OC?

In a perfect world you won't, but we don't live in a perfect world. You could accidentally activate your can while digging for it in your purse, your child could accidentally discover it. If you are like my poor long-suffering wife your husband may accidentally activate it while checking it for leaks…

A more likely scenario is that the wind blows some into your face as you actually use it, or a spray soaked bad guys spits and snots OC residue and you get it on you as you fight.

It really doesn't really matter HOW you got exposed. If you ever get OC in your face, your concern will be how to get it OFF.

Decontamination Protocol

If you have every misjudged just how hot your Nashville hot chicken actually was you know how soothing a big cold class of water is. Until you drink all the water and the burn intensifies.

What you need to know is that Oleoresin Capsicum is the *oily resin* of hot pepper.

Water doesn't do anything for OC spray either.

The idea that milk is a base and will soothe an acid burn is a good idea, except OC spray doesn't hurt because it is an acid so Milk does nothing either.

You need to get the oil off the body.

Dawn dishwashing soap is the most effective thing I have found to wash the oil off, but it is a little harsh on my eyes. Baby shampoo is what my experience finds to be the best option. It cuts oil well, and is gentle enough to pour directly on the eye, which is something I have seen people do.

Get some soap on your hands and lather it on the eyebrows, eyes, and the immediately adjoining facial areas. There is no sense in trying to wash the entire face. It is more likely that not that you will just spread the OC to you lips and mouth then get it all off.

Rinse the soap off.

Next, get out of the water. Seriously, get out of the water. I know you will not want to, I never want to either. While the cool water splashes your face you will think its helping. It isn't it is like that water at the restaurant. It is tricking you. True relief comes with time. As long as you are in the water you are not allowing the OC spray to deactivate.

Some rub the water off their face, those people tend to look red and puffy the next day as towels and rough scrubbing irritate the eyes. Personally I drip dry. It is easier, and at this point I am really not caring about how I look.

After you get out of the water the best thing you can do is take your fingers and pry your eyes open. You may think your eyes are swollen shut and it is not possible to open them. You would be half right. Once you get them open the first time, they will immediately shut. It will be easier to open the next time. Keep prying them open until you can open your eyes without your fingers prying them open. Once you can open them, regardless of how long you can keep the open, start blinking.

At this point blinking will be difficulty, but it will become easier.

Your goal is to rapidly "strobe" your eyes until they tear up. Tears are your goal. Blinking rapidly will cause tears to form.

Tears contain an enzyme that helps clear the eyes. This will work wonders for removing the last traces of the oleoresin.

You will be surprised how quickly rapid blinking will relieve your eye discomfort.

During all of this many people panic. If your attacker panics when he gets a face-full of spray then maybe you will help persuade him to find a new line of work. However, panic is makes the pain seem worse. Panic robs you of confidence and the ability to make good decisions.

Panic is the worse thing you can allow at this point. Luckily there are breathing exercises that both help keep you calm AND reduce the chances you inhale any pepper spray residue.

I find that with the soaping and blinking procedure above, the following breathing technique really helps with successfully dealing with an OC exposure.

This is called combat breathing, and while it is commonly taught in advanced self-defense courses, I first learned of it in Col Dave Grossman's book **On Combat**.[1]

The idea is to breathe in a cycle of 4, 4-second deep breaths in through the mouth, hold, and then breathe out through the nose for a 4 count. Repeat.

After a few cycles the deep oxygen exchange will tend to clear your head and calm you down. I know I do it when the boy acts up and I need to take a second.

An additional benefit from breathing out from the nose tends to keep you from inhaling any pepper spray residue.

It is of great importance not to get the two confused.

Last time I got sprayed I volunteered to go first and since my blinking got me workable pretty fast I went around helping my fellow students. I was loudly extolling the virtues of breathing and staying calm. "in through your mouth, out through your nose...." At some point I got twisted up and reversed the procedure. Well, I paid for my confusion as I sucked up a big blob of water/OC mix.

The pain of pepper to the eyes is nothing on what it is in the lungs. I almost gagged hard enough to vomit out my own toes...

In my defense, I failed the system; the system did not fail me.

Almost monthly I have former students tell me that the OC decontamination system "really works". They generally add that they thought I was just talking in class, and/or they took a while to try it in real life. Keep it in the back of your head, because if you ever get sprayed you will want to stay calm and get it off of you as soon as you can.

11

HOW TO DECONTAMINATE ITEMS

The following works, and works well. However, it is not for your personal decontamination of OC spray. It is NOT safe for use on your face or any sensitive areas.

In making **hot sauces** and other things that use hot peppers I am getting used to accidentally contaminating sensitive areas of my body with oleoresin capsicum.

If you have ever watched any of my **YouTube videos** on making hot sauce you might have heard me warning my help not to rub their eyes after using hot peppers. Without fail they always seem to get burned. It almost always happens after they wash their hands and think they have the hot pepper resin off of their hands. Usually the burning happens when they go to the bathroom.

I got tired of feeling guilty for laughing at my young non-listening nephew or getting in trouble by my pretty but non-listening wife. I decided to do some research to see how to cook with peppers without getting burned and the solution is actually pretty simple.

Hand Soap doesn't do much to remove the oleoresin capsicum from skin, generally only time works. Fortunately since it is an OILY resin it is possible to saponify it (turn the resin into soap).

Much like using sodium hydroxide to turn fat to soap calcium hydroxide (in bleach) can make the oil water-soluble.

If you mix a 10% beach solution using bleach and water and dip your hands in the solution from time to time as you are working with peppers it will make the resin into something close to soap. It will feel slippery but will rinse clean with water.

Once again, do NOT use the bleach on sensitive areas like your eyes or genitalia, and make sure you wash the bleach off very thoroughly.

Use common sense and I think you will be very pleased. The first time I tried this **I made a video of the process** and was very surprised it actually worked since nothing else seems to.

I tried this (well a version of this using a less caustic chemical) to get the same saponification process last time I got pepper sprayed for certification. The science was valid, it was well documented in a paper from the poison control center (using milk of magnesia), unfortunately it did not work.

I do know, from experience, and from the video above, that bleach solution DOES work on the hands and kitchen utensils to allow you to cook with peppers without getting burned.

It clearly removes the hot pepper oil off of surfaces. Once again for the record, DO NOT use it around the eyes or mucus membranes this method is for things not beings.

AFTERWORD

I hope this book was useful to you. I wanted a book that covered the basics, was easily understood, was not dull, and had very little fluff.

My wife says I am not a funny as I think I am, so some of my anecdotes may have not been as entertaining as I hoped, but regardless the information comes from years of experience.

How many people will let their **wife pepper spray them** so they can tape giving a basic pepper spray class while experiencing the burn of OC to the eyes? If this eBook wasn't enough information you can see me doing just that.

If you got anything out of this book I hope it was how important proper defensive mindset is to surviving attacks, that OC spray is a good tool when lethal force is not available or legally justified, that you need to practice carrying and using your spray, and that you can get exposed and not panic.

It should go without saying, but I will say it just to be clear. The information presented in this book comes from years of experience and formal training, but the opinions expressed are mine alone and do not represent any individual department or agency.

PLEASE REVIEW

Please visit my Amazon Author Page at:

https://amazon.com/author/davidnash

if you like my work, you can really help me by publishing a review on Amazon.

The link to review this work at Amazon is:

https://www.amazon.com/review/create-review?asin=B07BPLSQZK

ALSO BY DAVID NASH

Fiction

The Deserter: Legion Chronicles Book 1

The Revolution: Legion Chronicles Book 2

The Return: Legion Chronicles Book 3

The Warrior: Legion Chronicles Book 4

Homestead Basics

The Basics of Raising Backyard Chickens

The Basics of Raising Backyard Rabbits

The Basics of Beginning Beekeeping

The Basics of Making Homemade Cheese

The Basics of Making Homemade Wine and Vinegar

The Basics of Making Homemade Cleaning Supplies

The Basics of Baking

The Basics of Food Preservation

The Basics of Food Storage

The Basics of Cooking Meat

The Basics of Make Ahead Mixes

The Basics of Beginning Leatherwork

Non Fiction

21 Days to Basic Preparedness

52 Prepper Projects

52 Prepper Projects for Parents and Kids

52 Unique Techniques for Stocking Food for Preppers

Basic Survival: A Beginner's Guide

Building a Get Home Bag

Handguns for Self Defense

How I Built a Ferrocement "Boulder Bunker"

New Instructor Survival Guide

The Prepper's Guide to Foraging

The Prepper's Guide to Foraging: Revised 2nd Edition

The Ultimate Guide to Pepper Spray

Understanding the Use of Handguns for Self Defense

Note and Record Books

Correction Officer's Notebook

Get Healthy Notebook

Rabbitry Records

Collections and Box Sets

Preparedness Collection

Legion Chronicles Trilogy

Translations

La Guía Definitiva Para El Spray De Pimienta

Multimedia

Alternative Energy

Firearm Manuals

Military Manuals 2 Disk Set

ABOUT THE AUTHOR

David Nash has been a member of the firearm community for over 20 years. He is a firearm instructor trainer holding numerous certifications. David currently works full time as a correction academy instructor as such he teaches chemical agents, defensive tactics, electronic restraint devices, firearms, and how to deal with angry felons.

As a former US Marine, emergency manager, and experienced correctional officer Mr. Nash has learned that mindset, attitude, and command presence are more important than any particular tool or any specific technique.

He is a father and a husband. He enjoys time with his young son William Tell and his school teacher wife Genny. When not working, writing, creating content for YouTube, playing on his self-reliance blog, or smoking award-winning BBQ he is asleep.

amazon.com/author/davidnash

facebook.com/booksbynash

youtube.com//tngun

goodreads.com/david_allen_nash

twitter.com/dnash1974

instagram.com/shepherdschool

pinterest.com/tngun

NOTES

Introduction

1. https://www.tngun.com

1. What is Pepper Spray?

1. http://www.historyofwar.org/articles/weapons_metsubishi.html
2. https://www.smithsonianmag.com/history/forgotten-history-mace-designed-29-year-old-and-reinvented-police-weapon-180953239/

3. What is the Proper Mindset?

1. https://en.wikipedia.org/wiki/Tennessee_v._Garner
2. https://en.wikipedia.org/wiki/Graham_v._Connor
3. http://www.businessdictionary.com/definition/reasonable-person.html

5. What Type of Spray Should I Buy?

1. https://www.safariland.com/on/demandware.static/-/Sites-tsg-Library/default/dwd4ad6a29/resources/less-lethal/aerosol-reports/oc-and-pepper-sprays.pdf
2. https://www.sabrered.com/formulations-heat-strength-and-law

6. What Are the Laws on Pepper Spray?

1. https://www.atf.gov/resource-center/docs/guide/state-laws-and-published-ordinances-2010-2011-alaska/download
2. https://law.justia.com/codes/arkansas/2010/title-5/subtitle-6/chapter-73/subchapter-1/5-73-124/
3. http://consumerwiki.dca.ca.gov/wiki/index.php/Pepper_Spray_(Mace/Tear_Gas)
4. https://www.flsenate.gov/Laws/Statutes/2017/790.01
5. http://qcode.us/codes/kauaicounty/
6. http://www.legislature.mi.gov/(S(xghhgtxbpgbf2huldjzemhtk))/mileg.aspx?page=GetObject&objectname=mcl-750-224d

7. https://www.atf.gov/resource-center/docs/guide/state-laws-and-published-ordinances-2010-2011-nevada/download
8. http://codes.findlaw.com/ny/penal-law/pen-sect-265-20.html
9. http://lis.njleg.state.nj.us/nxt/gateway.dll?f=templates&fn=default.htm&vid=Publish:10.1048/Enu
10. http://apps.leg.wa.gov/RCW/default.aspx?cite=9.91.160
11. https://docs.legis.wisconsin.gov/statutes/statutes/941/III/26

10. How Do I Decontaminate Others or Myself?

1. Grossman, Dave and Loren W. Christensen. On Combat: The Psychology and Physiology of Deadly Conflict in War and Peace. 2nd ed. PPCT Research Publications, 2007

BONUS: EXCERPT SPANISH EDITION

Introduction

Si me preguntaras quién soy, respondería que soy papá. Ser un hombre de familia es el aspecto más importante de mi vida. Mantener y proteger a mi familia es lo que veo como mi mayor propósito. Afortunadamente, mi carrera me ha permitido reunir las habilidades y la información para poder proteger eficazmente a mi familia de las amenazas de la vida.

Como verás, soy un instructor de armas de fuego desde hace mucho tiempo, ex marine de los EE. UU. Y defensor de la preparación. He escrito varios libros publicados tradicionalmente sobre el uso de armas de fuego y la preparación para desastres. Este es mi primer libro autopublicado, pero he enseñado este tema durante casi 20 años.

Soy dueño de una escuela privada de capacitación llamada Shepherd School. Originalmente comenzó como una escuela de armas de fuego, pero a medida que crecían mis habilidades y certificaciones, también entendía lo que significaba proteger a mi familia. Las armas son solo un aspecto de la verdadera preparación y protección. Tengo que poder vendar una herida, enseñarle a mi hijo a mantenerse alejado de los problemas, saber cómo apagar el fuego de la cocina, hacer que mi familia se refugie durante una tormenta y cambiar una rueda pinchada. Ser el protector de la familia es más que solo poder emplear la fuerza letal. Tengo esa opción si necesito usar un arma, pero ¿qué pasa con aquellos que no pueden portar un arma de fuego o no quieren?

Mi esposa es maestra de educación especial. No podía llevar una pistola al trabajo incluso si quisiera. Ella no quiere hacerlo. A menos que alguien esté tratando de lastimar a nuestro hijo, no estoy seguro de que ella pueda disparar un arma contra otro ser humano. Escribí esto como una guía para personas como ella. Quiero darle una guía de calidad sobre cómo comprar, transportar, usar y descontaminar el aerosol de pimienta. No juzgo tus elecciones. Solo quiero ayudarlo a sentirse (y estar) más seguro.

He sido instructor de aerosol de pimienta durante casi 17 años. Mi primera experiencia con agentes químicos fue en 1993 cuando entré en la Cámara de Gas en la isla de París. Un año después, recibí mi primera dosis de aerosol de pimienta mientras trataba de impresionar a una chica, presumiendo. Tenía una pequeña lata que su papá le regaló cuando fue a la universidad, y quería mostrar cómo no era tan poderoso como las cosas que usamos en los Marines. Me equivoqué en ambas cuentas, ella no estaba impresionada y aprendí el poder de un buen aerosol de pimienta.

Más tarde me convertí en oficial de corrección y luego en instructor de agentes químicos. Con los años perdí la noción de cuántas veces me rociaron. Me han rociado mucho, ya sea para entrenar o como efecto secundario de luchar con alguien que está rociando, duele y no es divertido. Actualmente trabajo como instructor de la academia de corrección, y rociamos a nuestros cadetes como parte de su capacitación formal previa al servicio. Con el entendimiento que proviene de miles de exposiciones al aerosol de pimienta como la persona que rocía, haber sido rociado e ayudar a descontaminar a la persona rociada dentro y fuera del aula, por eso puedo decir con confianza que entiendo bien la mecánica del uso del aerosol de pimienta. También sé lo que no ayuda a que deje de doler.

También puedo decir que he escuchado casi todas las malas teorías concebibles sobre el aerosol de pimienta. Este breve libro está diseñado para separar los rumores de los hechos y dar el mejor consejo posible.

If you are interested in the Spanish version of the Ultimate Guide to Pepper Spray, you can find it on Amazon.

www.ingramcontent.com/pod-product-compliance
Lightning Source LLC
Chambersburg PA
CBHW031329250726
48656CB00005B/2041